The NAME of the GAME

*Making a Lasting
Connection with your Kids*

STEVE SCHALL

New Leaf Press

You have heard the expression, "He has a heart as big as he is." That's a great compliment for a guy who is 5'6" tall, but pin that one on a man who stands a full 7' barefoot, and you've described Steve Schall, the author of the book of the year for parents (my opinion, soon to be joined by scores of others). Steve has done it. He has raised four fantastic kids and helped hundreds of others through a rapidly growing national ministry where he presides effectively. Steve knows kids like the back of his massive hands, and if this book will help make kids anywhere close to as wonderful as Steve's kids are, you better buy a case of them and pass them out in the neighborhood.

Dr. Joe White
President, Kanakuk Kamps

As a state representative in the Arkansas General Assembly, Steve stands out, but for much more than his 7' frame! He is one of my most valued allies in the state capitol because he is one of those special people who get elected with a mission in mind. His mission is to sacrifice himself for the service of others, especially to serve the cause of the family and to hold high the ideals of real fatherhood. I'm not surprised that his book is so good — Steve wouldn't be able to do anything less than excellent. This is a great and compelling challenge to me to realize that of all the little titles and honors others bestow upon us, none ranks up there like the title that God himself entrusts us with — *Dad*. Steve has never stood taller.

Mike Huckabee
Governor, State of Arkansas

A mentor's responsibilities include passing on values; this is one of the things I learned from a great mentor, Mr. Henry Iba. Through my associations in the game of basketball, I've tried to impart to my players the things Mr. Iba and others have taught me, and it has given me much pleasure to see these things reflected in the lives of men like Steve Schall. When I coached at Arkansas, during the days of the Triplets and our first Final Four team, Steve stood out because I could see in him a future mentor to young people. Our lives intersected on a gym floor many good years ago. I'm glad we still agree about what's really important in the game of life.

Eddie Sutton
Head Basketball Coach, Oklahoma State University

Steve Schall is a tall man with a big heart. And this book demonstrates it. It is biblical, practical, sobering, and encouraging all at the same time. If you are a parent serious about connecting with your kids — heart, soul and mind — you need this book.

Dr. Stu Weber

The Name of the Game

First Printing March 2001

Printed in the United States of America

For information write to New Leaf Press, P.O. Box 726, Green Forest, AR 72638.
Please visit our website for other great titles: www.newleafpress.net

ISBN: 0-89221-492-9

Library of Congress: 99-069242

For information regarding publicity, please contact Dianna Fletcher at 1-870-438-5288.

We would like to thank the University of Arkansas in Fayetteville for use of their photos.

New Leaf Press

Dedication

To Debbie
Without whom I would never know the joy of fatherhood.
And to Christin, Taylor, Amelia, and Anna Catherine
May you run in such a way as to win the prize.

Acknowledgements

Any pretense of writing about the issue of parenting without first and foremost acknowledging the insights and example of my wife, Debbie, would be just that: a pretense. For almost a quarter of a century, Debbie has faithfully walked beside me, as we have together struggled through the ups and downs of trying to raise godly kids (a task, by the way, that we're still squarely in the midst of). I thank her for her strength and courage, and for the laughter and the spontaneity that she brings to my life and our family. Truly, it is just as the Lord declares: Her worth is *far* above jewels. Thank you for being a wonderful soulmate, both for this life as well as the one to come.

I also want to thank the K-Life leadership team, both those with whom I work on a daily basis, as well as the men who serve on our national board, to whom I report. Thank you, friends, for giving me the privilege of pursuing this project. May each of you be blessed to receive the rich heritage of a godly legacy, to the glory of the Lord Jesus whom we serve together!

And, to Christin, Taylor, Amelia, and Anna Catherine: You four are the only four people on this planet who call me "Dad," something that is both a wonderful privilege and a weighty responsibility. I love the way your hearts are increasingly reflecting the heart of the Lord. Plus, you guys are just plain *fun* to be with! Thanks for adding such joy to my life.

Finally, there are a few others whom I need to thank. Ken, for encouraging me to pursue this pathway, and prodding me along until it finally got done. Mark, whose regular accountability is more helpful than he knows. Tim, for putting up with more delays in getting this manuscript finished than any reasonable man would . . . *thank you* for not giving up on this project! And finally, Bob and Jeannette: The incredible beauty that surrounds your Colorado home proved to be just the inspiration that I needed to finish this. Thank you.

Steve Schall
Arrowhead at Vail, Colorado
March, 2000

By now we're all familiar with the story of the *Titanic*. More than likely you can readily recall the tragic love story portrayed through the Hollywood media machine. Girl meets boy, teenage emotion begins flowing, and love grows like crabgrass! The attraction between the two young stars seems unstoppable. Is this really a love story for the ages? Hardly. It's an image of tragedy that resulted from unmet expectations. The *Titanic* was touted as the "unsinkable vessel" utilizing a new technology of the time that separated the hull of the ship into 16 separate compartments. Each compartment was designed so that if the integrity of the hull was damaged, any water that leaked into the ship could be isolated in that one compartment. I can imagine there wasn't a person on that boat who thought they would end up treading water that night. But when the massive steel plates started creaking and groaning and the iron rivets started popping free from the hull, a shock wave of reality rippled through the mighty *Titanic*.

Parenting can be a lot like a ride on the *Titanic* at times. We set out thinking we're indestructible, only to find out how quickly our compartments are shattered and torn. Let's face it, we're all busy people these days, and there are endless demands on our schedules. Put up boundaries in your schedule, a hedge of protection around your time with your kids. For instance, many times I've been asked to lead a breakfast Bible study for businessmen in our city. But I've chosen to spend that time with my kids, studying the Book of Proverbs. As a parent, if you don't guard your time with your children, you can be sure that no one else will.

This book is a great place to start if you are looking for answers to the difficulties of parenting. The reality is, great parenting doesn't just happen, it takes a strong commitment to God's Word and a focused look at the issues we face in our culture today. As parents, we must be willing to get out of our comfort zone — to say "no" to the good in order to pursue the best — and look for opportunities to invest in our children. I think Moliére said it best: "Men are alike in their promises. It is only in their deeds that they differ." It's true that just like the *Titanic*, if you try to compartmentalize your life, you will truly run the risk of ruining the integrity of your family. As parents you already know it's impossible to say one thing and do another — your kids can see right through that. They need us to step up and be the genuine article through and through. That is what will ultimately make the difference in our culture and leave a godly legacy for generations to come. Let's face it, kids are tired of passive parents; are you willing to accept the challenge of being a parent your child can count on? Then start with reading this book and spending daily time with your spouse on your knees in prayer. I can guarantee you will not be disappointed with the results.

Dennis Rainey
Executive Director of Family Life

F orever these towns will be linked to the tragic unraveling of a youth culture gone awry. With each new incident, parents all over this country bow their heads in grief, and wonder if their community is next. And if their kids are safe. And what — if anything — they can do about it.

While the questions are many and the issues complex, there is perhaps a silver lining in this dark cloud hanging over our children. After decades of running from any suggestion that our problems are moral and spiritual in nature, there are some signs that this culture is finally coming to grips with the fact that what's happening to kids today has more to do with the *heart* than the *head*. In the midst of the tragedy, we're beginning to understand that knowledge and prosperity are not the answer . . . that, in fact, kids who are quite intelligent and who live in wealthy homes are some of the ones who are struggling the most.

Finally, it seems, we're realizing that parental involvement and interaction at a *heart* level — or the lack thereof — is THE key factor in our kids making their way through a confusing and dangerous culture. It has nothing to do with their zip code or clothing or skin color, and everything to do with the foundation that is laid during their formulative years. Throughout this land, parents are once more awakening to the need for real, meaningful, and spiritually enlightening interaction with their kids and their kid's friends. After all, children are "factory-designed" to make lasting, life-long connections with adults, *especially* their own parents. Without those relational ties, too many kids drift into dangerous waters . . . as evidenced in some of the horrific events that we've suffered through in recent years.

The Name of the Game | 7

But becoming painfully aware of a void that must be filled is one thing. Developing deep convictions, that lead to changes in how we choose to schedule our time and align our priorities, is quite another. As has been often said, the road to hell is paved with good intentions. Lots of parents *want* a good connection with their kids. Getting there, for whatever reason, is sometimes another story.

Not long ago I was coming home from a speaking engagement. By the time I arrived, everyone was in bed. I was still charged up from the evening, not quite ready for bed, so I decided to plop down in my favorite chair in the den and engage in that great American sport known as channel surfing. Like most men, I don't really care what's on . . . I care what *else* is on. So off I went, happily clicking away until I came across the face of a man I knew and respected: William Bennett. He was just being introduced on a late-night talk show, so I decided to stop the surfing and listen in on what he had to say. What happened in the next two minutes is something I'll never forget.

The talk show host was asking Bennett this question: "Since protocol demands that I introduce you by your highest title, and since you've held two cabinet-level positions in the previous administration, I'm a little confused. Here's what I need to know: Is your highest title "Mr. Secretary of Education" or is your highest title "Mr. Drug Czar"?

I'll never forget Bennett's reply. Without a moment's hesitation, he looked back at the host and said these words: "Well, if you want to introduce me by the highest title that I've ever held, then you're going to have to call me "Dad" . . . *because that's the highest title I ever have — or ever will — hold."* You could have scraped me out of my chair. Here was one of the power brokers of our nation,

a man who continues to have a great influence in the
culture . . . and he gets it. He flat out gets it. In fact, he
gets it in a way that gives me hope for the rest of us.

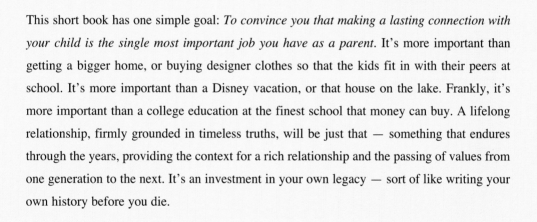

But even "getting it" isn't enough, not in this crazy culture.
We need more than that. We need *understanding* that leads to
positive change in the way we think about and interact with
our kids.

This short book has one simple goal: *To convince you that making a lasting connection with
your child is the single most important job you have as a parent.* It's more important than
getting a bigger home, or buying designer clothes so that the kids fit in with their peers at
school. It's more important than a Disney vacation, or that house on the lake. Frankly, it's
more important than a college education at the finest school that money can buy. A lifelong
relationship, firmly grounded in timeless truths, will be just that — something that endures
through the years, providing the context for a rich relationship and the passing of values from
one generation to the next. It's an investment in your own legacy — sort of like writing your
own history before you die.

But don't be fooled. Good, healthy relationships won't just "happen." They take time and
work, along with healthy doses of blood, sweat, and tears. And they demand an awareness of
the ways the culture works against you, as it tries to disrupt what God intended all along. As
awareness grows and convictions develop, you'll find in these pages practical advice that will
enhance your own creativity in making a connection with your kids.

Because in the end, a culture changes one life at a time. And kids who grow up secure,
confident, and connected in their relationship with their parents will be those who are most
likely to lead their own generation back to the moral and spiritual foundations from which this
country has drifted.

I could tell that it was going to be a problem at the very first practice, when Tommy (not his real name) kept cutting his eyes away from me as I was talking, looking nervously to the stands where his dad was seated. "Remember, guys — you listen with your eyes, not just your ears," I said in my best coaching voice, but I knew that there were issues with Tommy and his dad that would soon need addressing. Sure enough, at our first game, the pattern began. Dad in the stands, yelling at Tommy virtually every time he touched the ball. "Shoot!" "Watch Out!" "Get it!" And when Tommy made a poor pass, or threw the ball away (something every kid on the team did, without exception) there was the exasperated "Oh, Tommy!"

Since we weren't exactly in a sold-out gymnasium (this was Saturday morning basketball with 10-year-olds, mind you, with only their parents and a few close friends in attendance) the yelling stood out all the more. Tommy would look up at his dad every single time he made a mistake, or missed a shot. During time-outs, as I was explaining plays to the team, Tommy's eyes would continually cut away from me, to try and find out what his dad was saying to him.

Finally, I had to tell him — as gently as I knew how — that he had two choices. Listen to me, as his coach, and play and improve with the rest of the team; or listen to his dad trying to coach just his own son from the stands, and sit on the bench beside me. Mistakes were going to happen, I tried to explain, and it really wouldn't affect his future NBA career one single bit if he missed a shot or threw the ball away. Winning just wasn't that important; not nearly as important as developing his and his teammates' skills, and teaching him the character values that can only be learned through team sports.

But the scene I've just described is so common that we've come to accept it as "parenting in the new millennium." Let's face it. All of us live in the same culture — one that puts a high price on this thing called winning. Shirts with slogans like "Second Place is First Loser" abound, reinforcing the competitiveness that infects everything we do.

There's no question that some folks have it in pretty good perspective, and are able to accept both winning and losing with equal ease and grace. Increasingly, though, those people are becoming a rare and dying breed.

Instead, what we find is a growing majority of kids and parents alike who have bought into this cultural value system that celebrates winning above all else. Couple that with the fact that every contest tends to produce both a winner and a loser, and the stage is set for the kind of tension and strain that leads to "lost connections" with our kids. It's sort of like when the computer modem "times out" on you when you're trying to send an e-mail . . . all of a sudden you realize that there's nothing happening there.

Even that wouldn't be so bad — after all, learning to deal with defeat and disappointment is simply part of growing up, right? — if it were not for two additional factors that have converged upon us to muddy the waters.

The first has to do with the largest identifiable age group in the culture. They're the children of post-World War II, better known as the "baby boomers." They're also a generation that has enjoyed unprecedented affluence, while living through the most astounding technological and knowledge revolution the world has ever seen. To call them a generation of achievers would be a vast understatement. To call them "parents of teenagers" would be absolutely correct — for these 40-to-60-year-olds are now in the prime of their parenting years.

The Name of the Game

Having enjoyed success at virtually everything they've set their hands to do, boomers expect nothing less from their offspring. As Dr. Evelyn Thoman, a child development researcher at the University of Connecticut, points out:

"Baby boomers, who typically have enormously high expectations for themselves, tend to see every real or imagined flaw in their child as a sign that THEY have failed. They keep straining to create their fantasy of the ideal child, instead of appreciating the real child they actually have." [1]

Want to know how that plays itself out? Listen a little more carefully at the next kids' sporting event you attend. What you'll hear at a typical game are lots of parents "exhorting" their children — at the top of their lungs — to do those things that the child apparently has forgotten to value appropriately. "Get the rebound!" "Steal the ball!" "Don't let him score!" "Make a play!" Even those with "Type B" personalities — who would never dream of actually *saying* anything like that in a public setting — are harboring the same thoughts inside, anxious to see their child be the star.

As a veteran youth basketball coach, I've yet to come across a single kid who didn't *want* to get the rebound when he tried for it, or *want* to hit the shot when he took it, or *want* to play good defense when the opponent had the ball, or *want* to make a steal at a crucial point in the game. Fact is, *you don't always get what you want* — no matter how loudly your parents may be screaming.

If we're not careful, here's the message that communicates loudly and clearly to our kids. If they happen to win, we tend to congratulate them wholeheartedly, and bask in the glory of the conquest. It's a performance-based acceptance, good until the next time they take the court.

If they happen to lose, however — or even if they played poorly, but the team still won — it's another story. Then the message is typically communicated, in some form or fashion, that Junior didn't quite live up to expectations. Even though parents will try to sugarcoat it with "I'm proud of you" and "You tried your best" type of statements, most cannot resist the temptation to add their personal critique of the game. Including, in most cases, a fairly detailed assessment of how their child could have done better. The bottom line? The criticism has *far* more impact than *any* of the positive statements. Some studies suggest that a child needs to hear ten times as many positive statements as negative ones from a parent, in order to build healthy self-esteem.

The bottom line of this kind of parenting? Yet another step is taken in a direction *away from* a positive, connecting relationship between Mom or Dad and the child.

The same is true, by the way, for non-athletic activities as well — drama club, band, student council, even their performance in the classroom. In a culture that values high achievement above anything else, kids who are "just average" in a particular area — even if they excel in other areas — can struggle greatly with low self-esteem and self-acceptance. Isn't it interesting, as Dr. Howard Hendricks points out, that we "pray like crazy for our kids to be *normal* at birth — ten fingers, ten toes, two arms, one head — and then never, ever, *ever* accept 'normal' again, for the rest of their lives?" It is in the crucible of constantly failing to live up to what they sense are their parents' expectations that many children develop lifelong wounds, many of which never seem to heal.

Another way of saying it is this: Your child will *rarely* question *your* expectations. Instead, he will question *his own inability to live up to those expectations*. And when a child is unable to meet parental expectations, a lifelong quest to prove oneself worthy of the acceptance that is so desperately needed sets in. Good enough will never be good enough. And any chance of a healthy, connecting relationship between parent and child will be forfeited on the altar of continual striving for success and achievement.

A second factor that has caused us to lose the connection with our kids is perhaps even more damaging than the first — if that even seems possible. Somehow, we've come to equate sitting in the stands (or bleachers, or auditorium) and *watching* our child with those types of activities that actually *enhance* communication between parent and child. It's the same thing, really, as sitting around and watching TV. Fact is, in both scenarios, the communication is all in one direction, with little or no feedback or interaction. Not exactly a breeding ground for building lifelong relationships.

And even that could be overcome, were it not for the astonishing pace at which we tend to live our lives. Have time to sit around and talk after a game or activity, in a leisurely fashion, without the telephone, the internet, the television or the computer competing for our attention? Not in most households. Instead, our schedules are such that we often leave one event to rush to another, and then run home to get what we can done before falling in bed exhausted — so that we can get up and do it all over again the next day.

The losers in that equation, of course, are our kids. Sometimes I wonder if we wouldn't be much better served to let our kids go play the games or perform the concerts or act in the play with just their friends, free from our watching eyes and excessive expectations and our incessant need for them to perform. That way, we could save *our* time for real, meaningful interaction with them — the kind that would actually help shape their character and bless their lives.

Unreal expectations that damage the best of relationships. Time together that's not *really* time together. Both of these work powerfully against building the kind of relationship that kids need most from their parents. What's more, they leave us struggling to find common ground at a time when our kids need us most. And unfortunately, we're seeing that played out in the culture, in the form of "disconnected kids" who are wreaking havoc on institutions, like schools, that once were bastions of safety and sanctuary.

The very last verse in the very last chapter of the very last book of the Old Testament, Malachi 4:6, sheds some light on what we're living through. It's almost as though Mr. Malachi looked through a "time telescope" and saw our culture at the dawn of this new millennium. At the heart of the issue, he warned, would be the need for a lasting connection on the part of parents, *especially fathers*. And just how crucial would that be? How about "crucial enough to stave off a curse that could/would/might/IS running amok throughout the land?"

Beginning to gain a sense of just how important this business of building a relationship with our kids actually is? In the next chapter, we'll take a look at how our own background, personality, and gifting impacts the way we go about making — or losing — this crucial connection.

Endnote:
1. As quoted in the book *Different Children, Different Needs* by Charles F. Boyd (Sisters, OR: Multnomah Publishers, 1994), p. 30.

The Name of the Game

> *"Train up a child in the way he should go:*
> *and when he is old, he will not depart from it."*
> *- Psalm 127:4*

Years ago, Harry Chapin's song "Cat's in the Cradle" captured our national attention, with some of the most poignant lyrics ever recorded. The message cut to the collective soul of America, highlighting an all-too-common occurrence in the parenting process. Do you remember hearing these words for the first time?

A child arrived just the other day,

He came to the world in the usual way.

But there were planes to catch, and bills to pay.

He learned to walk while I was away.

And he was talking 'fore I knew it, and as he grew,

He'd say, "I'm gonna be like you, Dad.

You know I'm gonna be like you."

And the cat's in the cradle and the silver spoon,

Little boy blue and the man in the moon.

"When you coming home, Dad?" "I don't know when,

But we'll get together then.

You know we'll have a good time then."

My son turned ten just the other day.

He said, "Thanks for the ball, Dad, come on let's play.

Can you teach me to throw?" I said, "Not today,

I got a lot to do." He said, "That's ok."

And he walked away, but his smile never dimmed,

Said, "I'm gonna be like him, yeah.

You know I'm gonna be like him."

And the cat's in the cradle and the silver spoon,

Little boy blue and the man in the moon.

"When you coming home, Dad?" "I don't know when,

But we'll get together then.

You know we'll have a good time then."

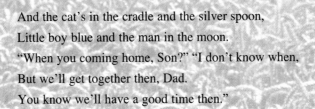

Well, he came from college just the other day,

So much like a man I just had to say,

"Son, I'm proud of you. Can you sit for a while?"

He shook his head, and he said with a smile,

"What I'd really like, Dad, is to borrow the car keys.

See you later. Can I have them please?"

And the cat's in the cradle and the silver spoon,

Little boy blue and the man in the moon.

"When you coming home, Son?" "I don't know when,

But we'll get together then, Dad.

You know we'll have a good time then."

I've long since retired and my son's moved away.

I called him up just the other day.

I said, "I'd like to see you if you don't mind."

He said, "I'd love to, Dad, if I could find the time.

You see, my new job's a hassle, and the kid's got the flu,

But it's sure nice talking to you, Dad.

It's been sure nice talking to you."

And as I hung up the phone, it occurred to me,

He'd grown up just like me.

My boy was just like me.

And the cat's in the cradle and the silver spoon,

Little boy blue and the man in the moon.

"When you coming home, Son?" "I don't know when,

But we'll get together then, Dad.

You know we'll have a good time then."

© 1974 Story Songs, Ltd.

Lyrics by Harry and Sandra Chapin

As Chapin points out in his sad, painful way, when left to figure it out by ourselves, *all of us* would revert — in some form or fashion — to the model of parenting in which we were raised. For those raised in traditional homes that upheld biblical values, that's a very good thing, one that speaks loudly of legacy and heritage. But for those at the other end of the spectrum, parenthood often brings more than its fair share of worry and anguish. What if we slip into old habit patterns that we learned early in life, and end up repeating the cycle? What if we don't have the skills or the knowledge we need to do it right? Or, what if we realize too late that we're missing something crucial to the parenting process, and end up leading our kids to the same destination that we find ourselves at, albeit through different pathways?

The real question that many of us are asking is this: Can we really and truly change our style when it comes to our parenting skills? Can we overcome deficiencies from the past, and adopt a new method and plan? And if so — how?

It's not much of a stretch to compare the task of parenting to that of coaching a team. Anyone who has ever coached, in any sport at any level, will tell you that meshing different personalities together to achieve a common goal is a *challenge*, at best. As a result, there are all sorts of approaches that coaches use to try and get their goals accomplished. Some like to yell and scream. Others tend to be more analytical, more emotionally detached as they coach the team, focusing on the "X's and O's" rather than on the people involved. Still others try the "friendship" approach, working to become more of a "buddy" with their players than an authority figure. And then there's the group that mixes and matches all the styles, so that you never know from one day to the next what you're up against. (Beginning to sound more and more like this thing called parenting?)

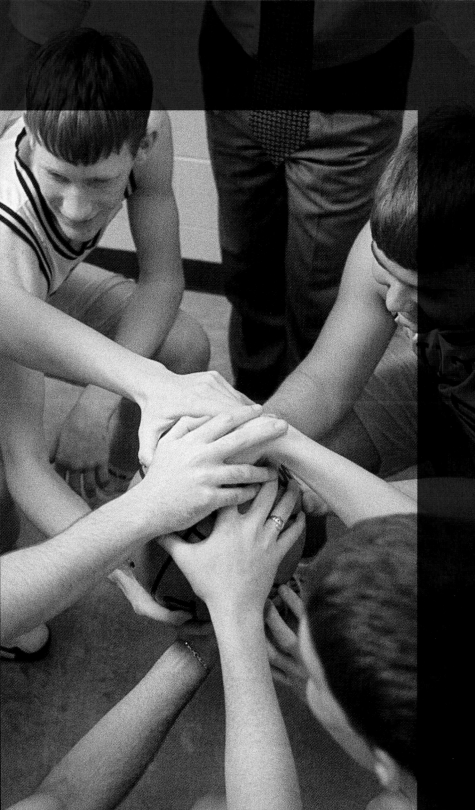

One helpful process for any parent (or coach, for that matter) is to take a long, serious look at the "style" that you tend to bring to the process of raising your kids. For example: Do you tend to be expressive and transparent, or more reserved and withdrawn? Are you given to a task orientation, with a "To Do" list for every day, or do you approach each morning as a clean canvas, waiting for the spontaneity of the moment to seize it and produce something unique and beautiful? Are you a person who needs to be in control at all times, or do you tend to allow things to develop at their own pace along their own course?

Your answers, of course, will help you determine what comes across to your kids as you parent them. My guess is that your own particular style has much more to do with how *you* were raised, than anything else. In much the same way that I tend to coach basketball the way that I learned it in college, with an emphasis on the "Three D's — Defense, Dedication, and Discipline" — so too do I tend to want to interact with my kids in the way I learned it while growing up. And, to carry the analogy a step further: Just as I've had to adapt my basketball coaching to accommodate the more up-tempo style of today's game, so too have I had to adapt my parenting style to a more interactive, relationally engaging approach, for the good of my own children.

And make no mistake about it. There *is* a particular "coaching style" that is *much* better than all the others, when it comes to making a lasting connection with your kids. Think of it as the "Eddie Sutton" or "Joe Gibbs" or "Phil Jackson" of all the styles . . . the one that will have the most long-term success attached to it, when the smoke clears and the dust settles.

One reason we know this is because of research done at the University of Minnesota by Professors Thomas and Gec, on the "Four Styles of Parenting." They were able to identify four broad categories that fit virtually every parenting style. The categories fit along an axis that ran from "low support" to "high support" and from "low control" to "high control." Each style fits into one of the four quadrants. The styles and their quadrant are illustrated in the following graph:

Think of the word "rules" when you see the word "control." And think of the word "relationship" when you see the word "support." Given your own style, background, and natural tendencies, can you figure out which quadrant you typically fall in, as it relates to your own parenting?

HIGH CONTROL
Lots of Rules

Authoritarian

Authoritative

LOW SUPPORT
Not Much Relationship

HIGH SUPPORT
Lots of Relationship

Neglectful

Permissive

LOW CONTROL
Not Many Rules

Here's another question: As you think this through, do you have a guess as to which parenting style *overwhelmingly* ranked "best" when studied for such outcomes as "produces kids who are able to withstand peer pressure" or "produces kids most likely to live out the value system of their parents"?

The answer probably won't surprise you. Without question, the very best parenting style, according to the study, is "Authoritative." Lots of rules, you bet . . . but lots of love and relationship to go right along with all the demands. These are parents who are actively involved in their kids' lives, willing and able to communicate not just the boundaries and rules, but also their love and affection.

The worst style, by contrast, was the one that shares a similar sounding name, but is in actuality worlds apart: "Authoritarian." That's the style that has tons of rules, but precious little interaction. Lots of laws, but very little love. And as someone once pointed out, "*Rules* without *relationship* is a breeding ground for *rebellion.*" Want to make your teenager really angry? Give him a bunch of rules to follow — such as where he can and cannot go, or whom he has permission to hang out with — without making any sort of emotional connection with him in the process. Laying down the law, without

The Name of the Game

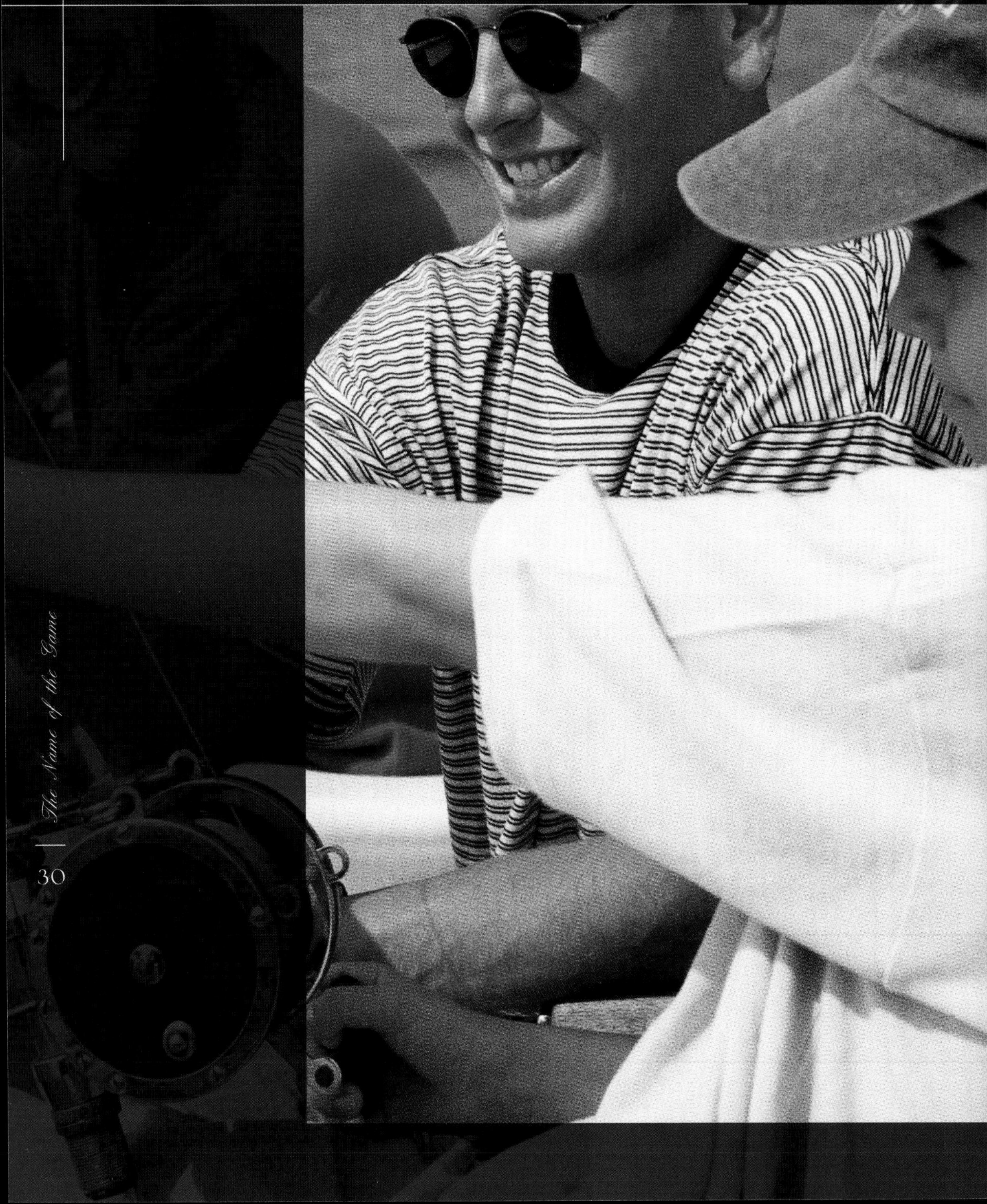

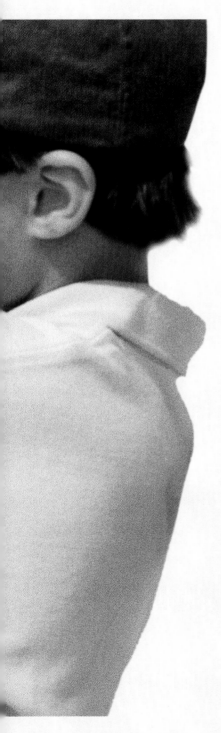

providing the necessary relationship that allows one to see the *heart* behind the lawgiver, is a sure pathway toward anger, rebellion, and broken relationships.

The next best style in the University of Minnesota study, by the way, is "Permissive: Low Control, High Support." Lots of love and relationship, but not as rigid with all the rules. These are the parents who say "bedtime is 9 p.m." but don't get bent out of shape if 9 p.m. turns into 9:30 or 10 or even 10:30, mostly because they are right in the thick of things with the kids anyway. By sharp contrast, those parents who don't establish any rules, but don't bother to invest in the relationship either, were the next-to-worst, with their neglectful style. At least they didn't stir up anger like the authoritarian group . . . but neither did they gain any ground from a relational standpoint, either.

The clear message of this study? Making an emotional, healthy, relational connection with your kids is *absolutely essential* to their ability to grow to maturity. If there's a side on which to err, it's most certainly the side that includes tons of relational time. Be authoritative, with lots of guidelines and rules, which give structure and comfort to a child, and provide order to his life. Or be permissive, with fewer rules but still the same amount of love and connection and relationship. Either is a step in the right direction.

Just how we do that, of course, is what the work of parenting is all about. And in the next few chapters we'll uncover several principles that will help us in this process.

CHAPTER FOUR

When I was in college, playing basketball for the Arkansas Razorbacks, our coach would often remind us of the responsibility that we had to be ambassadors to the state of Arkansas. Especially, he would tell us, as it related to the kids who looked up to us (pun intended). He even went so far as to have the following poem put up on the wall in our locker room, big as a power forward, where it was the last thing we saw before we hit the court for a practice or a game:

To A Razorback

There are little eyes upon you,
And they're watching night and day;
There are little ears that quickly
Take in every word you say;
There are little hands all eager
To do anything you do;
And a little boy who's dreaming
Of the day he'll be like you.

You're the little fellow's idol,
You're the wisest of the wise,
In his little mind about you,
No suspicions ever rise;
He believes in you devoutly,
Holds that all you say and do,
He will say and do, in your way
When he's a grown-up like you.

There's a wide-eyed little fellow,
Who believes you're always right,
And his ears are always open,
And he watches day and night;
You are setting an example
Every day in all you do,
For the little boy who's waiting
To grow up and be like you.

In today's culture, that seems just a tad out of place and old-fashioned. Take, for example, a Nike commercial by NBA superstar Charles Barkley from a few years back, in which Barkley pointedly told the other side of the story by staring at the camera and proclaiming "I am NOT a role model." (Personally, I couldn't agree more.) But his friend and fellow Dream Team member Karl Malone took exception, and made a point of telling him so, in an open and public letter printed in the "Point After" column of *Sports Illustrated*:

> I disagree with what Charles says in his recent Nike commercial, the one in which he insists that he is not a role model. Charles, you can deny being a role model all you want, but I don't think it's your choice to make. We don't *choose* to be role models, we are *chosen*. Our only decision is whether to be a *good* role model, or a *bad* one.

What's true for athletes is magnified a thousand-fold when it comes to parents. If you were to visit my son's room, for example, you might think that you had just entered the official "Shrine to Michael Jordan." His room is dominated by two huge, original oil paintings of Jordan performing his magic on the court, decked out in his Bull's uniform. Souvenir tickets and photos from a trip to the United Center, where we watched Jordan from courtside, add to the collection. There would be no doubt who the sports hero is for that boy, to any casual observer who entered the room.

But as much as Taylor might want to "be like Mike," Jordan's influence doesn't hold a candle to mine. I might not be able to beat Michael Jordan on a basketball court, but I can take him with both hands tied behind my back in the role model department, as it relates to how my kids respond and react to life. Jordan's influence, frankly, is one-dimensional and fleeting. His influence exists only at an

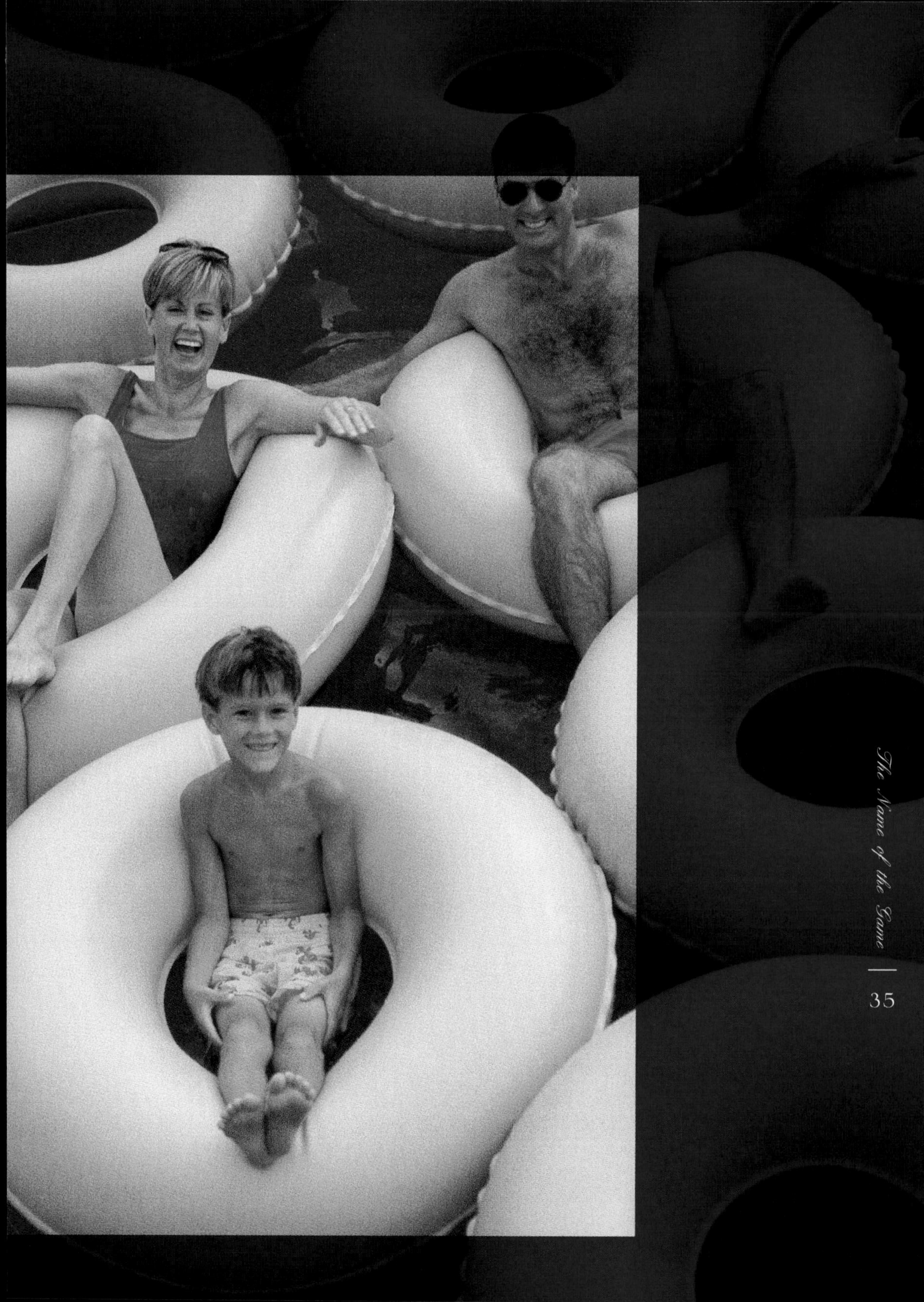

external level, in the area of athletics. And, honestly, his influence has to be marketed by Madison Avenue, in order to continue to work effectively. My influence, on the other hand, is multi-faceted and growing. It will continue to grow in both magnitude and scope throughout the years of his life, and needs no marketing gurus to help it succeed. Others will have a voice with which to speak into Taylor's life, no doubt. But no voice, and no example, will be as loud or as long-lasting as the voice and example of his father.

Make no mistake about it: God's plan and design is that truth would *be modeled and lived out on a daily basis* in front of our kids, in a way that allows our core values to be "caught" as much as they are "taught." You've heard the saying: "Kids would rather see a sermon, than hear one, any day." When it comes to communicating issues of lasting value, nothing could be more true. Or, for that matter, more important.

It's really no different than what God did for us, when He sent His Son. John's gospel reminds us that *"the Word became flesh, and dwelt among us, and we beheld His glory, glory as of the only begotten of the Father, full of grace and truth"* (John 1:14). Rather than leaving us to try and figure out the "rules" on our own, He gave us "relationship" in the form of the incarnation — the God-Man, Jesus Christ. In Him, we saw God as never before. In Him, we learned what it meant to live a life of total dependence upon the Father. In Him, we experienced life in all of its intended fullness and abundance.

And lest we forget: What we saw *first* of all was *grace*. *Grace* was what sent Jesus to us as a helpless infant in a forgotten stable in an obscure village in a Third World country, veiling His glory so that He might fully identify with us. *Grace* was what we beheld at every turn in His ministry, as time and time again He welcomed the oppressed and the downtrodden, the "tax-gatherers and sinners," into a relationship with himself. It was *grace* that *paved the way* for truth. In many ways, it is that same style of "incarnational ministry" that God is calling us to with our kids. As a friend of mine likes to say, our kids need to see "Jesus with skin on" — and the primary place that they are looking for it is from their parents. How does a child learn to be kind to others, tender-hearted, forgiving one another? How does a child gain the capacity to love others and respect them, regardless of their ethnic background or economic situation?

By watching his parents, that's how. I remember, for example, when our oldest daughter Christin was just five years old, at that highly impressionable age where everything seems magnified. We were living in Memphis at the time, and it was the day after Thanksgiving. As usual, my wife had prepared quite a feast the day before . . . at least enough to feed the entire block, or so it seemed. The leftovers were going to be "good eating" for quite a few days!

Until, that is, the garbage truck pulled up to pick up our trash. Debbie just happened to be looking out of the kitchen window, and she saw the guys rummaging through our garbage before they dumped it in the truck. When she saw one of them pull the turkey carcass out and place it in the cab of the truck, she couldn't stand it anymore. Out the door she went, arms laden with every bit of leftovers we had, insisting that those guys take it home to their families. She didn't think twice about it — it was simply her first response to the situation that was unfolding before her eyes, where she had an opportunity to meet an obvious need.

What she *didn't* realize, however, was how much Christin was watching every bit of this inter-action, and drinking it in. The reason I even know this story is not because my wife bragged about her big heart, or how she had done something so special or magnanimous . . . but because my five year old couldn't wait to tell me about it when I got home. The impact on Christin was profound, and to this day she has continued to have a compassionate heart, like her mother, for those in need. Not because she heard about it in a lecture or sermon — but

because she has seen it lived out, over and over, in her mother's life. The apostle Paul said it like this, when writing about his ministry with a church he planted in Thessalonica:

"Having thus a fond affection for you, we were well-pleased to impart to you, not only the gospel of God, but also our own lives, for you had become dear to us" (1 Thess. 2:8).

Do you hear the "connection" words in that verse? "Fond affection." "Well pleased." "We gave you our own lives." "You became dear to us." All of those phrases are wrapped, like soft blankets around a baby, around the timeless truth, "the gospel of God."

Give them truth, yes. But do it in the context of connection. Let them see the pure joy you have in being with them. Live out your values in front of them, in a way that lets them *see* the truth as well as *hear* it. And let grace cover all that you do, so that the truth is palatable and the connection is maintained.

Want to build a winning team in your home? It starts with realizing that God's intention is for truth to be *modeled*, first and foremost, and passed along in the context of relationship. Your kids will most likely do what *you* do, and when everyone is chasing the same goals, the team just gets that much stronger.

To do that successfully, however, means that you'll have to invest your most precious commodity — something we'll talk about more in the next chapter.

Years ago, as a young dad with a young wife and a young daughter and a young ministry, I was often faced with the realization that my greatest felt need was finances. Many times, there was "more month than paycheck" when it came time to pay the bills. Often, I found my faith being forged in the very real crucible of learning to trust the Lord for intensely practical things — like daily bread and groceries, for example — as our young family pursued the calling that we knew the Lord had set before us.

While things were tight financially, one of the great blessings of the job that I held was the fact that there were fewer demands on my time. Family memories from that "season" of our lives include plenty of fun family nights, lots of long, leisurely strolls, and more-than-my-fair-share of afternoons in the park, swinging and playing and laughing with that first-born daughter whom I loved so much (and still do to this day!).

Fast forward by almost two decades, and things aren't quite so simple. By no stretch of the imagination would I suggest that finances aren't still an issue in this family of six — we haven't won the lottery (or even entered it, for that matter) — but I am much more keenly aware that the single greatest commodity that I find myself in need of is not money, but TIME.

And I would guess that the same is true for you, as well. As the years roll along, life has a way of moving from the simple to the complex, from the "Christmas will NEVER get here" days of childhood to the "What? There's just three more shopping days until Christmas?!!" days of adulthood. Can you even *remember* those lazy afternoons, laying on your back in the grass, watching the clouds float by while trying to decide what animal they resembled? Can you believe that there was actually a time in your life when that kind of activity was a good picture of what your entire day looked like . . . no responsibilities, no worries, no pressure, no timetables, no schedule, no issues . . . nothing other than whatever struck your fancy in the moment?

In this hurry-up, instant-internet-connection world in which we live, memories like those seem to be a million miles removed. And not only do we experience it as adults, but our kids do as well. The hurried child, kids who are pressured to speed their way through childhood and adolescence, is no longer a cultural phenomenon, but an accepted fact. All of us — kids and parents alike — keep schedules that would have been impossible just a generation ago. And the impact of this frantic pace has been telling. Throughout all segments of the culture, time has become our most precious and important commodity. Our affluence has taken us down a pathway that rewards accomplishment and new paradigm shifts, while robbing us of what we need most. Make no mistake about it: Kids need time with their parents, *and lots of it*, to survive and thrive in this world.

Finding that time is one of the great challenges of parenting. Many of us have been wrongly influenced by the idea that it doesn't matter how *much* time we spend with our kids, as long as the time that we *do* spend with them is "quality time." But the reality is that the "quality time" vs. "quantity time" argument won't hold water. Kids do need quality time, no doubt. The only problem is that parents are never the ones who determine when quality time occurs. The kids are in the driver's seat on this one. So, it could be at Disney World, in the midst of a once-in-a-lifetime vacation. More likely, though, quality time will happen when you least expect it, like waiting for a tow truck to come after breaking down on the highway, or stopping at McDonald's on the way to school. Fact is, there's nothing special about the place. (Which may be the biggest, most costly mistake that parents make — we could actually save ourselves a lot of money if we learned this truth!) When kids are ready to talk, and unveil a window to their soul,

they will often choose to do so in the most unlikely places, at the most unlikely times. Parents are fooling themselves to think that they can control that process, and choose when and where quality time will occur. No, our only choice is to spend as *much* time as possible with our kids, realizing that *all* of our quality time is hidden — like a needle in a haystack — in the midst of our quantity time.

Which means, to be frank, that a large part of the parenting process becomes an exercise in self-denial, learning to say *"no" to the good* in order to *pursue the best*. For a limited period of time — around 18 years in most cases — we are given the opportunity to speak into and directly influence the lives of our kids. After that, our influence wanes. It's still there, of course . . . but it takes on a different form, and looks much more like an adult friendship than a parent-child relationship.

So here's the question. What are you doing now that's consuming major amounts of time, that can wait until later? Is it golf? The social scene? Work? Hunting? The internet? City or church leagues? Shopping? The list is pretty endless, and I'm certainly not trying to make the case that you shouldn't have a hobby or two. I *am* trying to make the point, however, that you *cannot* do it all. You *will* have to make choices. And the wise parent is the one who makes the right choice in the proper season, realizing that you

won't always be at this same
stage of life with your kids,
where your impact and influence
is so profound.

One of my favorite stories from
the Scripture is the account of
two sisters who had a deep
friendship with Jesus. Martha was the sister with whom every "Type A" personality can
identify with — she made a list, worked her list, and if it wasn't on the list, it probably
didn't get done. Mary, her sister, was at the opposite end of the spectrum. She was a free
spirit, more interested in people and relationships than she was in accomplishments and
achievements.

One time (see Luke 10:38–42), Mary and Martha were hosting Jesus and His entourage
during a pivotal time in the Lord's earthly ministry. Martha, in her usual fashion, was
trying to get the "stuff" done, to meet the needs of the crowd that had assembled. Mary,
in *her* usual fashion, was sitting at the Lord's feet, captivated by the things He was
saying, drinking in the deep sense of being in His presence, hanging on every word. The
more Mary sat, the more bothered Martha became. There was a lot to do! And it wasn't
going to get done if everyone just sat around and talked.

Of course, this passage is the "life-verse" section of the Bible for every free spirit. As
Martha got more and more exasperated with Mary, she finally took her case to the Master.
"Would you *please* tell Miss 'Spiritual' to get her bones in the kitchen, to help me with

the preparations for all of these people?" she asked Jesus (a bit of a loose translation, but I'm pretty sure that's close to how the original Greek says it). To which Jesus replied: "Martha, Martha, Martha, Martha! You're all hot and bothered by a bunch of nitpicking, little stuff, and yet only one thing is absolutely necessary. And Mary, for her part, has chosen the best pathway."

Not exactly the message that Martha wanted to hear, no matter how compassionate the tone of Jesus' voice may have been. Frankly, there's not a Type A in the world that would want to hear that message. *But we all need to*. And not only do we need to *hear* it, we need to *heed* it . . . especially as it applies to the time that we spend with our kids. The demands of life will always be tugging at us — that's a given. How we *juggle* those demands, and where we choose to spend our time, is a decision that only *we* can make. And yes, it will almost assuredly mean giving up something we truly love, or postponing a lifelong dream, in order to spend time with those kids who so desperately need us. But the great joy is that in so doing, we more fully reflect the Master, who himself laid aside the glory of heaven in order to spend time with us, showing us firsthand what it meant to walk in utter dependence upon His Father. Fact is, *anything worthwhile requires sacrifice*. And in this case, the price to be paid is well worth the cost invested.

The older I get, the more I am realizing that "The List" will *never* get done. Finish one project — this book, for example — and it will quickly be replaced by another task or assignment. Get better organized, use better tools to increase productivity, surround yourself with the finest assistants — both personal and digital — and you *still* are forced to come to grips with the cold, hard reality that you (and everyone else on the planet) have been granted a finite number of hours in each day. No amount of money can buy more time, nor add length of years to your life. We all have the same 24 hours a day to spend.

So the question becomes thus: How are we going to spend that time? Or perhaps the better question, as parents: What are the hard choices we're going to make in order to adjust our schedules to accommodate the very real "connection" needs of our kids? What are we going to postpone to another point in our lives, in order to invest that time in plain-old-fashioned "hanging out" with our children? How are we going to ensure that we have plenty of *quantity* time with them, so that we might be privileged to reap the reward of *quality* time?

It won't just "happen." It will demand hard choices and tough decisions. But then again — isn't that the price of true legacy?

"Fathering is a marathon, not a sprint."
- Paul L. Lewis

PROMISES, PROMISES

CHAPTER SIX

> *Dad taught me eveything I know. Unfortunately,*
> *he didn't teach me everything he knows.*
> *- Al Unser, Jr., U.S. auto racer*

A few years back, a movement swept our country that could only be described as the wind of the Spirit blowing through the culture. A football coach in Colorado, in the midst of his own painful family issues, invited a few hundred men to a meeting in Boulder, to examine together what it would look like to live godly lives as dads and husbands, leaders in their families and their culture. Those few hundred men turned into a few thousand the next year, then tens of thousands the following year, until hundreds of thousands of men from every corner of this country were examining themselves in light of God's calling to be men of their word. Somewhere along the way, the name "Promise Keeper" was hung on the organization, more as a way to remind the men involved of just what, exactly, they were being called to do: Keep your promises. The ones you made at an altar, when you promised in sickness and in health, for better, for worse, 'til death do us part. And the ones you make on a daily or weekly basis, as you interact with your wife and kids. Bottom line: Be a man of your word. Regain the ground that we've lost in this culture. Make it so that once again, a man's word is his bond.

Which, it turns out, is not as easy as it sounds when you consider the world in which we live. When the definition of truth gets parsed by our highest elected officials until we can't even find a question to ask that would help us discover what really happened, and when everything is relative with few or no absolutes, things can get real confusing, real fast. Even for those of us who want to do it right. Seldom will we have a problem with the big decisions, where things typically are a little clearer and well-defined. No, our issues will be in the thousand and one little decisions, in the daily stuff of our lives, as we try to live out the promises and commitments that we've made to those with whom we live and love.

When it comes to our kids, one of the best things to remember is that they simply don't have the same context for understanding life that we do. Along with the wrinkles and gray hair and extra pounds that middle age brings our way comes something called *perspective* . . . which is, understandably, completely lacking in the heart of a child. To them, a promise we've made to an outing or activity of any sort — a movie, a ballgame, throwing the football in the backyard, going shopping, taking a hike, going to the pool — is simply that: a promise. *A promise that was made to be kept.* And that promise can become the *absolute focal point* in the heart of a child, of any attempt we might make to connect with them at a given point in time.

Here's what we often fail to realize: We might have *very* legitimate reasons for not being able to follow through on a commitment or promise. Perhaps the boss called and added something to our plate that was unexpected. Or we had to take an emergency trip. Or we're not feeling well. Or a friend has an emergency need that can't wait. Or the car broke down. Or there's not enough money in the checking account. Or whatever . . . you fill in the blank.

But the fact of the matter is, our kids simply don't get it when the excuses start. Not because they don't love us, or are incredibly selfish little hellions. No, it has more to do with the fact that they have no *context* for the situation. They don't know what it really means to feel the weight of living in an adult world, trying to keep all the plates spinning without any of them crashing down around us. Nor would we want them to,

certainly not during their childhood. But it is that very lack of maturity and perspective that keeps them from understanding us, at any deep level, when we have to back down from a commitment we've made. And that, in turn, leads to a broken connection — any way you slice it.

Hollywood has made this point on several occasions for us, perhaps none better than the Jim Carrey movie *Liar, Liar*. Carrey plays a divorced dad who shares joint custody of his young son with his ex-wife. Dad makes promises to the son, and then proceeds to break them with predictable regularity (albeit with great style and flair, along with some world-class excuses). His ex-wife tries to pick up the pieces and help their son understand (which, of course, he never does, no matter how real or creative the excuse). Things come to a head when dad promises to attend the boy's birthday party, but doesn't make it. Finally, after waiting for several hours, the son realizes that Dad isn't coming after all. As moms will do, an attempt was made to salvage the situation, so a cake blazing with birthday candles was set in front of the boy, with everyone there encouraging him to make a wish and blow them all out.

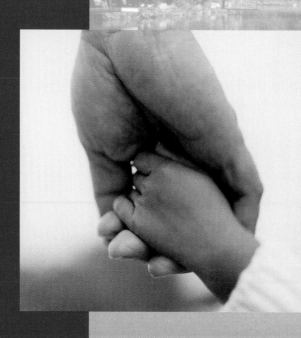

The wish that the son made?

That for a whole day, his dad would be incapable of telling a lie.

Stop and let that drip for just a minute.

The rest of the movie is a quite funny account of what a lawyer (Carrey's profession in the movie) who cannot tell a lie goes through in the course of a day. Without necessarily endorsing the entire movie, let me strongly endorse the moral of the story.

When dads can't lie to their kids, things start changing. Just like they did in the movie, with Carrey's character getting back with his son's mom at the end. And just like they will in real life, when dads (and moms!) begin realizing how important it is to keep their promises with their kids.

We do ourselves a great disservice when we fail to take into account how our kids, especially age ten or younger, process and assimilate information. Without the maturity to add a context, all they *can* focus on is what we say. So when we speak, we need to choose our words carefully, to keep the connection alive and growing. And when we promise something, we need to make sure that we're willing and able to follow through, barring a dire emergency. Doing so on a consistent basis will have the added benefit of bringing feelings of security and love to the heart of a child.

But making a connection by keeping our word means more than just the fun stuff. It also means that we're willing to keep the connection alive with our kids by keeping our word when it comes to discipline and correction . . . something we'll explore further in the next chapter.

> *"Whom the Lord loves, He disciplines."*
> *- Hebrews 12:6*

For the longest time, I was baffled by that verse from Hebrews. How could "love" and "discipline" go together? As a young Christian, I thought of love as that wonderful place of leaning on the everlasting arms of the Lord, where one was immune from the junk of this world. When I thought of discipline, it seemed to be at the exact opposite end of the spectrum, where anger and cruelty and yelling and screaming were the order of business.

I thought about incidents like the one from my wife's childhood, where her abusive father played out his cruelty one day during a family walk, taking a doll that my wife and her twin sister were arguing over and placing it on a nearby railroad track in front of an oncoming train, where Debbie watched in horror as it was smashed to smithereens. Discipline? Not hardly. More like child abuse.

When you grow up in a home like that, often your response to the word "discipline" is to equate it with the word "punishment," and run as far as you can in the opposite direction, vowing to never, ever, ever treat your kids like that. But in actuality, the two words are quite different. "Punishment" looks at objectionable behavior with vengeance, vowing to inflict harm of some sort on a person as the payment for that behavior. "Discipline," on the other hand, looks at objectionable behavior with great love, vowing to do whatever it takes to help change the behavior and shape the character, for the good of the person being disciplined.

When our first child Christin came along, my wife and I learned firsthand about how "love" and "discipline" not only *could* go together, but in fact *needed* to. After our first few years of trying the "no punishment" approach, out of reaction to our own childhoods, we found that we were raising a monster. Literally. With no boundaries to constrain her, Christin quickly learned how to control our lives, 24 hours a day, seven days a week. When things didn't go her way, she simply threw a temper tantrum, and we were left trying to do the parenting equivalent of walking on water: reason with a three-year-old. Talk about futility — we might as well have been flapping our arms and trying to fly to the moon. We were exasperated at every turn, frustrated most of the time, exhausted from trying to keep pace with a child who had a never-ending supply of energy and creativity.

Finally, in our desperation, we began looking for help — and came across a book that literally changed our lives. In fact, it's safe to say that, next to the Bible, this book has had the greatest impact in our lives. Nothing else has even come close.

The book? A new parenting philosophy by a little-known medical doctor from California, that took on the "no discipline" approach that prevailed at that time in our culture. *Dare to Discipline* by Dr. James Dobson became a life-saver for us, as our thinking about discipline was challenged and stretched. No longer did we see discipline as something to be avoided at all costs. Instead, we began to see and understand how discipline plays a critically important role in the parent-child relationship, helping to bring security to the child and peace to the parents, while enhancing and building the connection.

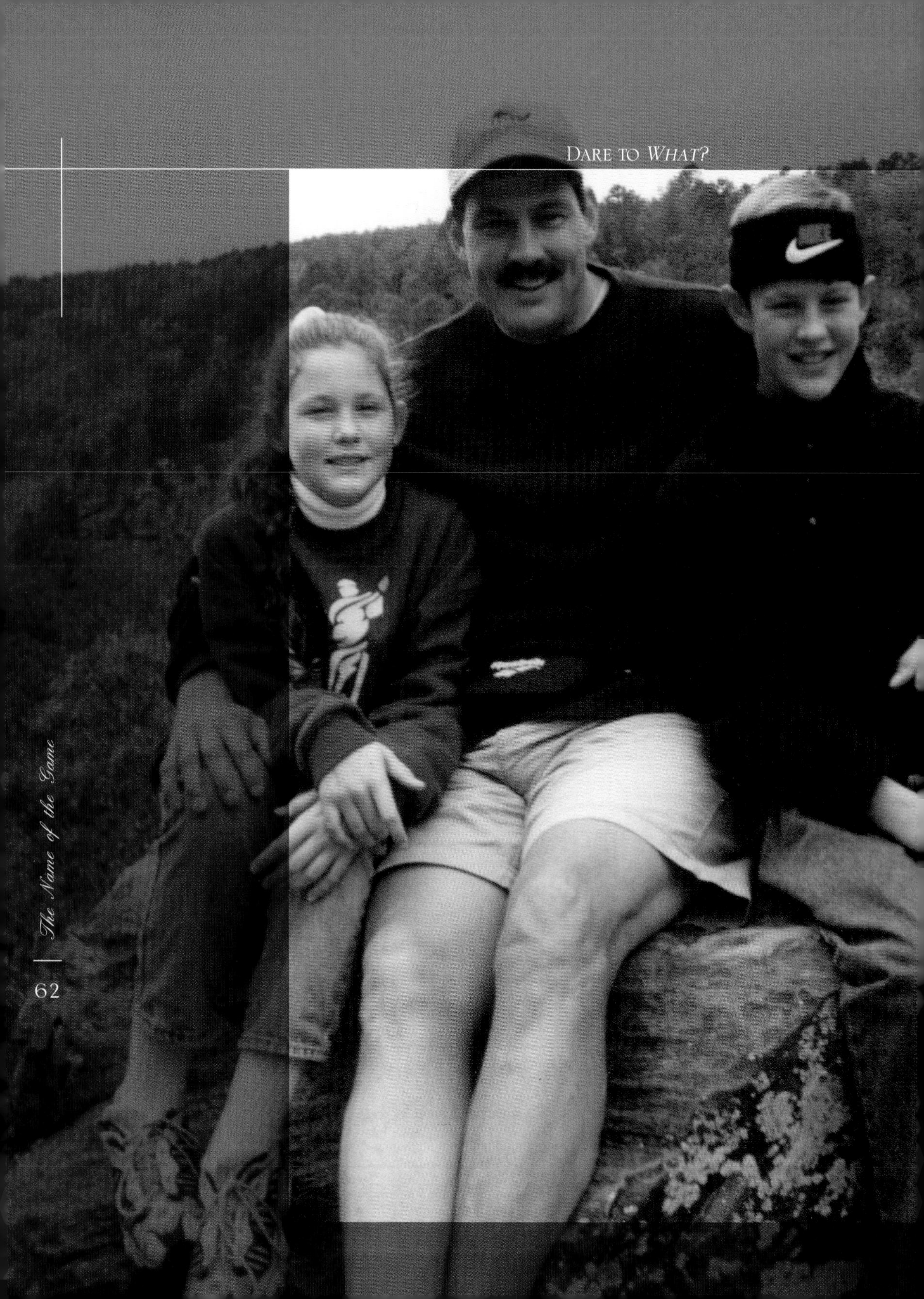
NIKE

But understanding is one thing. Trying to actually *apply* what you learn is quite another. After all, we were almost four years into this parenting process, and change didn't come easily. Christin was firmly entrenched at the center of our family universe, and dislodging her was not going to be easy. For almost two full years, we battled wills on a daily basis. Sometimes I wondered if Debbie and I would have the strength to go through another day of full-contact parenting. We could count on it: As soon as we established rules and boundaries, Christin would relentlessly test them. When we were sure that she understood the rules, and was willfully disobeying, we would discipline — often by spanking, with a wooden spoon — since that seemed to be the most effective tool in our "disciplinary toolbox" at that age in Christin's life. Often I would wonder how many times in one day I could spank this child. Two times? Three? Four? The record was five.

Slowly, though, the tide started to turn. Over a period of weeks and months, Christin finally got to the point where she knew that we meant what we said. And when that happened, the most remarkable change occurred. No longer did she test every boundary in every direction. Instead, this once out-of-control toddler began to adjust and live within the boundaries that we had set (for her own good, I might add!) and life became much more pleasant for everyone involved.

To this day, even as a college student, Christin has demonstrated the ability to live within the constraints of the boundaries that all of us must deal with on a daily basis. While many of her peers were struggling with rebellion during their teenage years, Christin has been able to successfully navigate through those times, confident and secure in both her place in our family, as well as with the convictions that our family holds. Convictions, by the way, that are becoming her own as she grows and matures.

My best explanation for Christin's relatively smooth pathway through adolescence is to look back at the war that was going on during toddlerhood. Seems to me that the best advice I can give parents is to win the battles, decisively, while the kids are young.

Win the battle then, and you'll be more likely (not guaranteed, of course, but certainly more likely) to not have to fight as many battles, or in as intense a way, when they get older.

But you can't "win" in an abusive way, of course, where kids are made to feel like the servants to the Lord and Lady of the Castle. Rather, the goal is to connect with your kids in a way that says, "This rule is for your own good, and because I love you SO MUCH, I'm going to help you obey it."

Let me give you a couple of examples. Studies show that kids who eat properly are much healthier, and better able to learn, than their counterparts who have poor nutritional habits. Since mealtime is often a battleground for parents, you might want to have a rule that basically says "You have to try it before you decide you don't like it" and another that says "If you don't eat your vegetables, you can't have dessert."

Enforcing those rules will actually be of great benefit to your child, whether they seem to think so or not. Regardless of their opinion on the subject, it's up to you, as the parent, to carefully draw the boundary line and make sure that both the expectation, as well as the consequence, are clearly communicated.

Or take bedtime — another major battleground in many homes. There's probably not a kid alive who hasn't resisted his bedtime. If your kids are anything at all like ours, they come with only two settings: On (full speed ahead) and Off (wouldn't wake up if a bomb exploded). Sometimes, it's a bit difficult to get the switch to shift from the former to the latter. But since we know that they need sleep, we set a regular bedtime that will accommodate that need. But then comes the choice *we*

have to make. Will we enforce that bedtime? Or will we let it slide, until it begins to erode our child's confidence that we actually mean what we say? Sadly, too many of us are all too often willing to let the boundaries slide. We get tired, busy or distracted . . . sometimes all three at the same time. And in the process, we take another step backwards, away from a connecting relationship with the kids.

Or perhaps we *are* willing to enforce the boundary. Maybe the scenario plays out like it has in our home: a bedtime ritual that includes brushing teeth, saying prayers, and loving words. Lights out, door closed. Ten minutes later: "Daddy, I need a drink." "Okay, but this is the ONLY time you're to get out of bed, until morning. You've had your only warning. If you decide to get up again, Daddy's going to have to get the spanking spoon, to help remind you to obey." Lights out, door closed. Ten minutes later: "Daddy, I'm hungry." Now what? After all, hunger is a legitimate need, isn't it?

Well, of course it is . . . and so are all the other things that we'll hear out of their cute little precious lips. While you may have to pause long enough to think through whether or not you actually fed them dinner, the reality is that in most cases this is a young child's way to test the boundaries. Did you really mean what you said? Could you *really* spank an adorable little bundle like me, just because I got out of bed when you told me not to?

The answer *has* to be yes. Not in anger, or in any sort of an overreacting way. Rather, with great love *and* great firmness. In our home, it would often involve a dialogue like this: "I'm so sad that you didn't listen to Daddy, and obey him. Remember how Daddy said that he was going to have to get the spanking spoon if you got out of bed? Well, now we're going to have to have a spanking, and that makes Daddy sad. But, Daddy wants to help you to learn how to obey him when he tells you something." And after the spanking, while holding the child through the tears: "Why don't we pray, and ask Jesus to help you obey Daddy when he asks you to do something. Wouldn't you like that? Remember, Daddy has to obey Jesus when Jesus asks Daddy to do something, just like you have to obey Daddy."

Here's my contention: When we as parents are willing to get out of our comfort zones, and involved in the disciplining of our children, we lay the groundwork for a connection at a deeper level than we could even imagine. If your children are young, and you can win the battles now, by all means do so. *That single decision will do more to help smooth out the road ahead for that child than almost anything else you could possibly do.*

And if your children are older, and reading this has caused you to realize that you haven't done all that you should have when they were younger, don't despair. *It's always the right time to start doing what's right.* Decide where the boundaries need to lie, and begin to establish them by first communicating your great love to your child, and acknowledging that you have let some things slide, in an unhealthy way. Tell him that you love him way too much to continue parenting like that. Try to help him understand why you feel the way you do. And then: Enforce whatever consequence you decide if he chooses to violate the

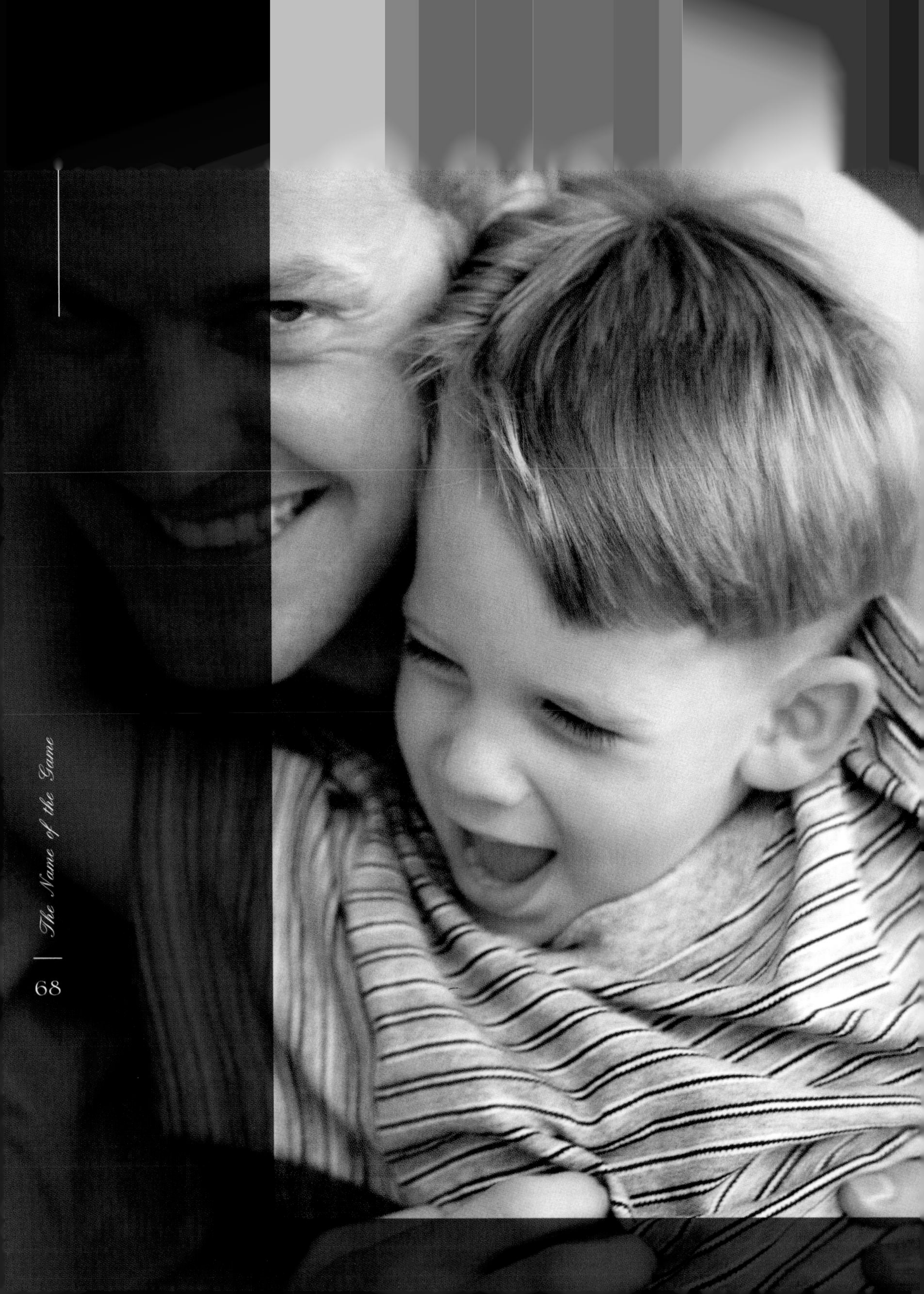

rule. If you want him home at 10:00 on school nights, and you've told him that violating that rule will mean that he loses his driving privileges for a week, then you *must* follow through with the discipline when he tests the boundary. Notice, by the way, that I said "when" not "if" . . . because you can be assured, 100 percent of the time, that a child who has grown accustomed to little or no rules and boundaries *will* test them when they get set in place.

But you want to know what else will happen? If you remember to keep "relationship" at the heart of your parenting, and do everything you can to reach out and love and communicate with that child, even as you establish boundary lines that have been non-existent, then you can be *assured* that you will be building into the security, confidence, and self-esteem of that young man or woman. Want to know the message that he'll be hearing, loud and clear? "Mom and Dad love me enough to care about what I do, where I go, and whom I hang out with."

But be realistic: Few and far between are the teenagers who will be able to communicate that message back to you. In fact, it may be years before you see the results of adding discipline to your parenting skills. Persevere! Fact is, *it's always the right time to start doing what's right*. And besides: Your kids *will* turn 30 one day, that magical age when one can begin to process his childhood . . . and when they do, the reward for fighting the good fight now will be evident and clear.

Discipline. Love. Connection. Like a three-legged stool trying to get by with only two legs, you can't really have one without the others.

Bear Bryant's Three Rules for Coaching:
1) *Surround yourself with people who can't live without football.*
2) *Recognize winners. They come in all forms.*
3) *Have a plan for everything.*
    - Bear Bryant
    U.S. football coach

LET THE ARROW FLY

CHAPTER EIGHT

> "Like arrows in the hand of a warrior, so are the
> children of one's youth." - Psalm 127:4

S everal years ago, Stephen Covey wrote a book entitled *The Seven Habits of Highly Effective People*. It instantly became a best seller, as people tried to glean the insights that it offered to those who wanted to accomplish more (in other words, just about everyone in this society). One of the habits that Covey highlights has had a profound impact on how I approach my life, and especially on how I approach the work of parenting. It's so simple that it's profound: Begin with the end in mind.

Makes you want to say what our teenagers love to say, doesn't it? "Well, duh!" As though that's not something we could have figured out on our own.

Or is it? How many of us have looked down the road, around the next bend, to see what's ahead for our kids? How many of us have really stopped to think through what we hope our kids will look like, in terms of their character and core values, when they are 20 or 30 years old?

The first step is to identify the end result (or the target, if you will) toward which we hope to send these little "arrows" that God has entrusted us with. The goal of every arrow, after all, is to strike the target toward which it is launched. One of the best steps toward "proactive parenting" is to take some time to determine just what, exactly, is the target for a particular child. I'm not talking about *what* they do. Whether they're a doctor, a missionary, a teacher, or a ditch-digger is not the issue. I'm talking about *whom they are* in *whatever* they choose to do. Their character. Their core values. Their world view. How they interact with and relate to others. What it is that motivates them. How they spend their resources.

All too often, I can allow the hectic schedule and pace of our busy lives to crowd out the time it takes to sit down and take an honest look at where the kids are currently, and where Debbie and I are praying that the Lord will take them.

Rather than being stuck in "wishful thinking" land, allowing the culture and peer pressure to unduly influence these "arrows in flight," my goal is to proactively guide them to several "release points" that will enable them to stay on track, bearing down on the target that God intends for them.

The process starts, really, with a careful observation and understanding of your child. Since every kid is unique, some will struggle in one area and excel in another, while the very opposite might be true for a sibling.

Take Taylor and Amelia, our two middle children, for example. Although they favor each other in looks (easily identified as brother and sister) and actually have a good friendship with one another, they also have major differences in how they are wired. Amelia is outgoing, gregarious, very social, and extremely verbal. She tends to communicate at a rate of about 300 words per minute, with gusts up to 500. She's the type who never met a stranger, and is typically in the middle of the action with her peers. The more friends, the merrier.

Taylor, on the other hand, is more quiet and withdrawn, more apt to observe and study a situation before weighing in with his opinion. He likes to plan, is very well organized, and has a pretty clear idea of where he would like to head in life. He tends to spend most of his time with a few close friends, and is motivated by adventure trips, basketball, and other fun activities. Since he's figured out that adventure trips can be costly (snow skiing, for example) he is also motivated by his allowance and other ways to earn money. He may be the only 14 year old that I know of who has a pretty good grasp of 401(k) retirement plans and the stock market.

Amelia couldn't care less about finances. If she has money, she'll likely spend it if she comes across something she wants or likes, or perhaps give it to you, if you asked her for it. It's just not a big deal to her. What gets her attention are her friends.

Taylor, by contrast, is quite content to be alone, either shooting baskets or reading a book, or perhaps building an Excel spreadsheet on his computer that will amortize his allowance over the next three years, so that he can see how much he'll have to earn for the Alaskan adventure that he is currently scheming about. Having friends over is not the end of the world to him. What gets his attention is what's in his wallet.

Here's the point: There's no way that Debbie and I can approach these two children in the same way, *even if the target toward which we hope to release them is very similar*. Amelia will have one set of tools that are useful in shaping her character, while Taylor will be influenced and shaped by quite another set of issues. Even though the target may be almost identical, the way they are released toward that target must, by necessity, look quite different.

For example: I remember seeing the trends in Taylor's personality begin to emerge a few years ago, when he was eight years old. There was nothing that he liked better than home, with the entire family gathered around. For Taylor, that brought great feelings of warmth, love, and security.

But part of growing up is learning to function in a nurturing environment away from the family, too, so we made the decision to send Taylor (along with older sister Christin) off to one of the best Christian camps in America, Kanakuk Kamp. We spent a lot of time with Taylor prior to the big "drop off day," assuring him of our love and reminding him about all the fun and adventure that he would have there at Kanakuk. The big day came, and we dropped him off in the midst of a great, fun atmosphere there at Kamp. Then, after checking to make sure that Christin was okay, and arranging for Amelia to stay with friends, Debbie and I headed out of the country for a short-term mission trip.

Five days later we were back at our home, going through the mail that had been piled up on our kitchen table while we were

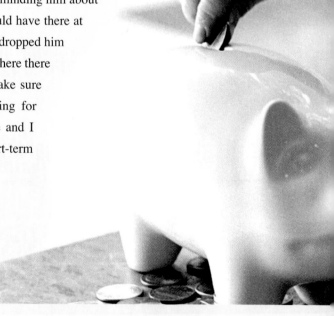

away. Of course, there were the requisite letters from Kamp, from both Christin and Taylor. Being the "Type A" personality that I am, I sorted the letters (there were five from each child) by postmark date, and pushed Christin's stack of letters across the table to Debbie, while I opened Taylor's. While Debbie took in glowing reports from Christin about how Kamp was going, here's what I read:

Well, I reasoned, that's just his first day. Being wired the way he is, it will just take him a little longer to get used to things there. So, I picked up and opened the second letter:

Now I was beginning to wonder whether we had done the right thing. Maybe he just wasn't quite ready to grow in this area of relating to others beside his family. What if we had missed it, big time?

Pushing aside those thoughts, I reached for the third letter in the stack, and began to read:

Well, that about did it for me. Just as I was reaching for the phone to call Kamp, Debbie suggested that I first finish reading the last couple of letters. So, somewhat reluctantly, I picked up the fourth letter and found this:

Dear Mom + Dad,
Kamps Great!
I Love you a lot!
Geuss what. I was the only person to get a gold K in high jump! We had our looney tune party! It was a blast!
SCOTT IS COOL!
Love,
TAYLOR

I must admit that I laughed out loud when I got to that fourth letter. And, the fifth one was similar, as were all the rest of them until we arrived at closing ceremonies to pick up this boy who had turned the corner after the third day (as Scott the counselor put it) and had the time of his life (as Taylor put it).

Looking back, that Kamp experience was a major turning point for Taylor. Like his father, he still prefers home to just about any other place on the planet. But he has also grown by leaps and bounds in his ability to relate to others and gain joy from building relationships outside of the family . . . a skill that he'll need, as he flies toward that target that God has for him. And Amelia? She would never struggle in a setting like Kamp . . . that would simply be contrary to her God-given nature.

Her issues are more likely to be those things that Taylor excels in. Different kids, different temperaments, different needs. Similar goals, similar pathways, similar results. Beginning to see how important it is for us to find those "release points" that help launch each unique child toward the target?

And, to be honest, the process doesn't stop until our kids are well into adulthood. All along the way, there are plenty of opportunities to speak into the character development and growing maturity of our kids, by how we choose to "let out the string" on these high-flying kites. Puberty is a release point, as we help our kids understand their sexuality in a healthy, biblically based way. Getting their driver's license is another. (Letting them take the car out by themselves is still another!) So is graduating from high school, and starting college, and living apart from the family for the first time, and getting married, and getting that first full-time job (to the cheers of parents everywhere!). All along life's pathways, there are all kinds of places to proactively speak into the development of your child's character and values. Opportunities to affirm, to exhort, to correct if necessary, to help point out the way.

In other words: opportunities to let the arrow fly. Do it well, and more often than not, that arrow will strike at the heart of the target to which it was launched. And with enough arrows flying toward targets of character and world view and spiritual values, who knows? We might just see this culture turn around and begin moving back toward its former foundations.

Leaders aren't born, they are made. And they are made just like anything else, through hard work. And that's the price we'll have to pay to achieve that goal, or any goal.

- Vince Lombardi
U.S. football coach

MAKING THE CONNECTION

A few years back I decided that our family needed a good opportunity to bond together, so I decided to embark on a sure-fire plan for wholesome family interaction. We went camping.

Understand that I am somewhat "outdoor challenged," so as I was planning this activity, which the family got totally pumped about, I realized that I had a few items that we still needed to pick up . . . minor details, like a tent and sleeping bags. Off I went to our local sporting goods store, in search of just the right thing. And boy, did I find it. They had this tent there that even I, all seven feet of me, could stand up in! Just the perfect item, I decided . . . it had a foyer, two back bedrooms (I'm not making this up) and even a declaration on the box that it "sets up easily in just ten minutes." Who could ask for more?

Well, the weekend for the big trip came, and off we went. At least I had the foresight to invite some good friends along, with their two small kids and his outdoors expertise. We arrived at the campsite, and in about three minutes he had set up their dome tents . . . it took two of them for their family, since they were just two-person tents. We, on the other hand, took almost two hours to figure out how the 143 poles that came with our tent fit together, much to the amusement and heckling of our good friends. While we set up the tent, they cooked dinner. Finally, we had the thing up, and we all sat down to eat . . . only to find that the dark clouds that had been gathering all afternoon were, indeed, full of rain, which proceeded to fall on our heads at the picnic table. Not to worry, though . . . we simply gathered up our plates and made a mad dash for OUR tent, where all nine of us had a delightful time over dinner in the foyer . . . we never even had to open the bedroom flaps. For that matter, we could have set up either of our friend's tents inside our tent's bedrooms . . . that's how huge this behemoth was.

The rain signaled a front that was moving through, so of course we all just about froze to death that night. Then, when we got up the next morning to cook breakfast we found the dog our friends had brought with her snoot in the pancake batter (a great diet plan, actually . . . makes you "not hungry" at a moment's notice!). And on and on this story goes . . . if it wasn't one thing, it was another. Not exactly what most people would consider a "successful" camping trip.

But you know what I think? I think it was actually a quite successful trip. Not from an outdoors perspective — I'm sure that true woodsmen are still chuckling at our rookie mistakes. But from the standpoint of pulling our family together, and making a memory that we share over and over and over again, it couldn't be beat. We have laughed until there are tears running down our faces, thinking about that weekend! And each time we relive it, we cement our family legacy just that much more.

Let me ask you this: What are the things that you are doing, to help you hand off your core values to the next generation? What are the special memories that just your family has together? What makes you unique and different, and helps you stand out from the other six billion people on this planet? How are you celebrating special holidays in such a way that your kids gain a sense of being uniquely called to your particular family unit?

How you answer those questions will have everything to say about your legacy, as well as about what you can expect when you enter your grandparenting years. Kids who develop a deep sense of identity from their family are much more likely to pass along not only those traditions, but also the core values that accompany them.

Someone said it like this: Raising godly, well-adjusted kids, with whom we have made a lasting connection, is like writing your own legacy before you die. Frankly, I couldn't agree more. When our kids know that we have a long-term view of things, and are already starting to think and pray about our grandchildren (and, by inference, their future spouse), then another plank in that foundation of security and connection gets laid in their soul. At the very least, it communicates to them that we aren't going anywhere . . . that the scourge of divorce that has plagued this nation is not a card we're holding up our sleeve, "just in case things don't work out." At best, our ability to speak about the "generations yet to come" gives our kids a heightened sense of their own importance in being all that God has intended for them to be, as they carry the timeless truth of the Gospel from one generation to the next.

Just how that happens, of course, is what this book has been all about. There are no secret formulas when it comes to good parenting, no guaranteed steps that will apply to every child. Each kid is so

unique and different that it would be ludicrous to think that the complex work of parenting could be reduced in such a way! Rather, there's a set of solid, wise, biblically-based principles to follow, and a God who desperately wants you to succeed to guide you, every hour of every day.

Finding your way, with *your* kids, is a journey that only you can take. Others can help to encourage you, and enlighten you, and even walk along beside you. But only *you* can make the deep connection with your kids that they are God-designed to receive.

So in the end, it comes to this: May the Father of our Lord Jesus Christ — the one who knows well what it means to parent a "less-than-perfect" flock — grant you the courage, the desire, the wisdom and the endurance, to make a lasting connection with your kids that will survive for all eternity.

That, indeed, is *The Name of the Game*.

"Children are not casual guests in our home. They have been loaned to us temporarily for the purpose of loving them and instilling a foundation of values on which their future lives will be built."
- James C. Dobson

Recommended Reading

Raising a Modern Day Knight by Robert Lewis

Parenting Today's Adolescent by Dennis and Barbara Rainey

Different Children, Different Needs by Charles F. Boyd

The Way They Learn by Cynthia Tobias

in the
PAINT

Disco fever. The Bee Gees. Long lines at the gas pumps. Fresh memories of Watergate. Shag carpeting. *Orange* shag carpeting.

Remember the seventies?

I do, but for a very different reason than those listed above. The last half of that decade found me in one of the greatest tension points of my life.

To be sure, there was much in my life to enjoy as a member of an Arkansas Razorback basketball team that was well on its way to making an indelible mark on the history of the sport in our state, reaching heights of success previously thought unattainable. With increasing success came increasing visibility, both in the state as well as nationally. And with the increasing visibility came the almost daily lectures from our head coach about the responsibility we had as athletes to be good ambassadors and worthy role models for the kids whom we would influence everywhere we went.

And therein was the tension. On the one hand, I knew that I wanted to live up to the expectations that were being placed upon me, both in how I performed on a basketball court *and* in how I lived my life off the court. On the other hand, I knew that my ability to live up to those expectations were worlds apart: *On* the court was one thing — I could always work harder and play smarter and do my best to fit in as a team

player; but *off* the court, I knew that my character simply didn't measure up to the expectations. I felt, as Garrison Keillor once described, like the proverbial "bear riding a bicycle — he can be trained to do it for short periods of time, but he would rather be out in the woods, doing whatever it is that bears do there." In much the same way, I knew that I lacked the self-discipline and moral convictions to be worthy of being followed by anyone, much less kids who were choosing their own pathways for life. I could do it for short periods of time, but I quickly reverted to the lifestyle I had always known — a life that was lived apart from God and His purposes, focused on "whatever felt right at the time." Hardly a role model for anyone, that's for sure.

In the midst of the tension, however, I made some interesting observations. Several of my teammates lived lives that were noticeably, distinctly different from mine. When most of the team would grumble about early morning practices, for example, they would keep a level countenance and endure. When their performance on the court didn't measure up to expectations, they would avoid the pits of despair that I often found myself in during similar experiences. Slowly, over a period of time, I began to realize that they had something that I was missing. Just what that was, however, I couldn't quite put my finger on. Perhaps it was their family background, or maybe just the way that they were wired. It all seemed so elusive and confusing to this 19-year-old college student, trying to navigate my way along life's pathway.

One of them in particular, Marvin Delph, tried his level best to convince me that what he had that I didn't was simply a "personal relationship with Jesus Christ." Having been raised as a sporadic-at-best Episcopalian, I wasn't buying it. By the time I got to college, I was convinced that all religion was for the weak-minded, and that there were serious intellectual issues with Christianity, especially. As far as I was concerned, King James had

The Name of the Game

re-written the Bible to make it say whatever it did for his own political reasons, and it was an outdated and obscure book that could not possibly have any implications for life in the modern era.

After the impossible task of trying to argue me out of my firmly held, "right-in-my-own-eyes" convictions, Marvin finally gave up trying. Instead, he took a new approach. He gave me a copy of a book entitled *More Than a Carpenter* written by a man named Josh McDowell, who had been down a very similar pathway in his own experience with Christianity. "Your arguments don't make any sense," I remember Marvin saying to me, "and until you read this book, I'm not even going to talk with you about this anymore. After you've read it, we can talk again."

Of course, in my arrogance, I equated Marvin's approach with near-victory on my part. Having argued him into a corner, I reasoned, I would finish him off with his own material. After several weeks of being asked "Have you read that book yet?" every time I saw Marvin, I finally took the time to settle down with it, on a Friday night in October of 1977. *I'll just skim through this so that I can needle Marvin some more* I thought to myself, as I picked up the book. Never in my wildest imagination did I suspect that God would have other plans.

To be completely fair about what actually happened that night, I must tell you that I was *not,* in any way, shape, or form "looking for God" that night. I didn't believe the Bible was anything more than an ancient book. I wasn't in some emotionally distraught state of being. I didn't think that I needed whatever the Church had to offer (not that I even really knew, or even cared to know, just what the Church was all about). And I most certainly wasn't interested in becoming some kind of "religious freak." I just wanted more material for my arguments with Marvin, getting his requirement for resuming the debate out of the way so that I could taunt and exasperate him all the more.

But God had other plans.

I shall never forget it. As I picked up the book, it was as though I entered a place where time was suspended and distractions were kept at bay, and all of my senses were at full alert. I read the first chapter of this simple paperback, which set the stage by recounting McDowell's own journey towards faith, and what he had discovered along the way. I remember being amazed at the correlation between his pathway and mine, as chapter after chapter raised the very same objections that I had to Christian faith, only to find good, solid, logical answers waiting as I turned the pages. By the time he presented C.S. Lewis' classic argument regarding the three choices an individual has when confronted with Jesus: 1) that is, to call Him the greatest *liar* of all time (He *knew* He wasn't God, but just claimed to be), 2) to call him the greatest *lunatic* of all time (He actually thought he was God, on the same level as a man who thinks he's a poached egg), or 3) to fall on your knees and call Him what He called himself — Lord *of* all time, I was ready

to believe. My heart had turned to God well before I got to the very end of the book, where McDowell presented a simple prayer expressing a desire to know Jesus Christ personally.

As soon as I put the book down, my very first thought was, *I need to read the Bible!* A few years earlier, a Christian teammate from my high school team had given me a copy of *The Living Bible* as a graduation gift. Of course, I had no interest in reading it at the time, but I

thought that it might be bad luck to throw away a Bible, so I had packed it with some other stuff and carted it off to college, where I left it in a box in the top of my closet (while, incidently, I proudly displayed my bright red "Buddha Statue" on my desk!). I jumped up and went rummaging for the Bible, and when I found it, I realized I had no idea where to start reading it. So, I simply took it and started to read from where it fell open . . . Romans chapter one.

Along about the time that I got to verse 20 or so, I thought I might be a candidate for a heart attack. My heart was racing, as I read the words "professing to be wise, they became fools instead, and exchanged the glory of the incorruptible God for an image in the form of corruptible man. . . ." *That's ME* I thought, *That's exactly what I have done!* Yet, even as the conviction deepened, so too did the sense of being forgiven for my foolishness and pride, for the sin that had caused me to think that I could actually figure out life apart from God. An incredible sense of His grace and mercy covered me, as His love permeated my soul. To begin an evening with no thought of God, and to finish it converted by His truth and His love is a marvelous experience, indeed!

The weeks following my entrance into the Kingdom were, as I look back, almost funny in terms of how things played out. Since I had experienced such a dramatic "Paul-on-the-road-to-Damascus" conversion, with nobody around to witness it, other Christians weren't quite sure what, exactly, had happened, nor how to interact with me. I think some may have wondered if one can legitimately come to Christ without someone sitting down and leading them through a presentation of the Four Laws!

For my part, I discovered University Baptist Church on the edge of campus, and thought that surely this was a place where God

himself resided, so clear and true and challenging was the teaching from the man we called, "The Rabbi of the Razorbacks", Dr. H.D. McCarty (who has faithfully served as pastor of that church for over 30 years). That church, along with organizations such as the Fellowship of Christian Athletes, served to help ground me in the faith that I had once resisted, and now embraced with every fiber in my being.

I write these words almost a quarter of a century after the events I've just described, yet the truth I embraced as a young college student is just as fresh and vigorous in my soul now as it was then. Have I lived a perfect life since coming to Christ? No. One would have to go no further than a conversation with my wife to discover that. But has the direction of my life, and the pathways I've pursued, changed as a result of this encounter with the Living Christ? You'd better believe it. And nothing, I think, is more important or dramatic than the change that this conversion has brought to my parenting.

In much the same way that I was powerless to live the kind of life that my college coach was calling me to, as a role models for kids, apart from an inside-out change of heart, so too are we all, as moms and dads, powerless to truly make any sort of lasting connection with our kids apart from the *power* that a relationship with Christ supplies. In some ways, it is as futile as trying to drive a car with no engine. Sure, we can pretend we are getting somewhere, and make believe that things are okay, from an "appearances" standpoint; but only an encounter with the Living God can give us the power that we need to actually get moving in the right direction.

To that end, my prayer is that you, too, will find the truth that sets you free — free to make a lasting, eternal, and God-honoring connection with your kids.

"Children are God's apostles, day by day sent forth to
preach of love, and hope, and peace."
- James Russell Lowell